10 Game-Changing AI Skills That Will
SHAPE YOUR FUTURE

*What You Must Learn Now to Lead in the
Age of Artificial Intelligence*

Alejandro S. Diego

Copyright © Alejandro S. Diego, 2024.

All rights reserved. No part of this publication may be reproduced, distributed, or transmitted in any form or by any means, including photocopying, recording, or other electronic or mechanical methods, without the prior written permission of the publisher, except in the case of brief quotations embodied in critical reviews and certain other noncommercial uses permitted by copyright law.

Table of Contents

Introduction: Embracing the Age of AI 3

Chapter 1: Prompt Engineering – The Power of Asking Right.. 6

Chapter 2: AI-Powered Personal Branding – Standing Out in the Digital World............................. 12

Chapter 3: Data Storytelling and Visualization – Turning Data into Narrative.. 20

Chapter 4: Creative Intelligence Automation – Unlocking Your Creative Potential with AI............... 26

Chapter 5: AI Strategy and Execution – The Key to Business Success... 34

Chapter 6: AI Project Management – Overseeing the Future of Innovation... 45

Chapter 7: Natural Language Processing (NLP) – The Language of AI... 57

Chapter 8: Continuous Learning and Curiosity – The Mindset of AI Leaders.. 66

Chapter 9: Understanding AI Limitations – Navigating Pitfalls and Risks...................................... 77

Chapter 10: AI Ethics and Policy – Shaping the Future Responsibly.. 91

Conclusion.. 106

Introduction: Embracing the Age of AI

In today's world, artificial intelligence is no longer a distant concept reserved for science fiction. It has seamlessly integrated into our daily routines, influencing how we work, live, and even think. The rapid shift in technology, particularly AI, has reshaped industries on a massive scale, making its presence felt in sectors ranging from healthcare to finance, education to entertainment. As AI continues to evolve, it's not only transforming large corporations and technical fields but also touching the lives of individuals in ways previously unimaginable. Tasks that once required manual effort are now handled by machines in a fraction of the time, while decision-making processes have become more data-driven and efficient.

This monumental shift presents both an opportunity and a challenge. On one hand, those who can harness the power of AI stand on the cusp of unprecedented possibilities. On the other hand, for those who lag behind, the gap between them and the future grows wider each day. It's no longer a matter of simply keeping up with the latest tools or trends—mastering the right AI skills has become an essential part of staying competitive in any field. The speed at which AI technology is advancing demands a new level of adaptability and awareness, one that requires individuals to not only understand how AI works but also apply it creatively and strategically in their personal and professional lives.

These ten AI skills are not just technical proficiencies; they are the key to unlocking a future where you can thrive, not just survive. From understanding the intricacies of AI-powered tools to mastering the art of prompt engineering, these skills offer a roadmap to positioning yourself ahead of the curve. Each skill directly impacts how you operate within this new AI-driven landscape, providing tangible benefits that extend beyond mere productivity. They influence how you interact with technology, communicate ideas, and even how you brand yourself in an increasingly digital world.

In this era of rapid competition, those who possess a deep understanding of these essential AI skills will have a distinct advantage. While many are struggling to keep pace with the transformation AI brings, those who dedicate time to mastering these abilities will rise above 98% of the population that remains unprepared. The competition isn't just among businesses or industries anymore; it's personal. As AI continues to integrate into more aspects of life, those who are equipped with the right knowledge and tools will stand out, leading the charge into the future while others struggle to catch up. By taking the initiative to learn and apply these skills, you secure not only your relevance but your leadership in the ever-evolving AI landscape.

Chapter 1: Prompt Engineering – The Power of Asking Right

Prompt engineering is the process of crafting specific and precise inputs, or prompts, to effectively communicate with an AI system, ensuring that it delivers the desired output. Think of it as the skill of asking the right questions in the right way to get the most accurate and useful responses from an AI model. Just like a conversation with another person, the clarity and structure of your question will determine the quality of the response you receive. In the case of AI, especially with models like GPT-4, the wording, context, and detail in the prompt can dramatically influence the relevance and accuracy of the answer.

In the AI world, prompt engineering has become an indispensable skill, not just for developers or tech experts but for anyone who interacts with AI tools. This includes content creators, marketers, entrepreneurs, or even casual users experimenting with AI for personal use. The better you are at constructing prompts, the more efficiently and effectively you can harness the power of AI. It is not simply about telling an AI to perform a task—it's about guiding it in a way that aligns with your objectives.

The significance of prompt engineering lies in its ability to unlock the full potential of AI. A vague or poorly constructed prompt can lead to confusing or irrelevant outputs, wasting time and diminishing the value AI can provide. On the other hand, a well-structured prompt allows AI to generate content that is focused, coherent, and aligned with your goals. Whether it's generating ideas for a project, automating a process, or analyzing complex data, the right prompt can make all the difference in the output AI delivers.

By mastering prompt engineering, you gain control over AI systems, allowing you to leverage their capabilities to the fullest extent. This not only saves time and effort but also ensures that you are making the most out of the AI tools at your disposal, putting you at a distinct advantage in a world where efficiency and precision are key.

The way you frame a prompt can drastically affect the quality of the output you receive from an AI system. Even subtle changes in wording, structure, or specificity can be the difference between receiving a general, vague answer and getting a detailed, focused response that precisely meets your needs. Let's consider an example. If you were to ask an AI to "write an article about dating apps," you would likely receive a broad, unspecific result. The AI might cover a wide range of topics, from the history of dating apps to user statistics and trends. While this might be useful in certain contexts, it's not particularly targeted.

Now, imagine reframing that prompt more precisely: "As a relationship expert, explain how dating apps benefit men in their 30s." Suddenly, the AI is guided toward a very specific goal, allowing it to generate content that is much more focused and relevant. This minor adjustment in phrasing tells the AI not only the topic but also the perspective and specific audience you're aiming for. The difference is night and day—the second prompt leads to a more meaningful and useful response because it narrows the scope, giving the AI clear instructions on what's expected.

This principle applies across a wide variety of tasks. Whether you're asking an AI to generate a blog post, summarize a report, or even brainstorm new ideas, the more precise and structured your prompt, the better the output. Vague prompts result in general and often unhelpful answers, while clear, detailed prompts direct the AI toward producing content that's aligned with your objectives.

One of the most exciting aspects of prompt engineering is that it's not a skill reserved for tech professionals or AI developers. You don't need to have a deep understanding of coding or AI systems to benefit from it. In fact, it's a tool that anyone, from business owners to content creators, can use in their daily work. Let's say you're a freelance graphic designer. You could use AI to generate content for your portfolio by asking it to "create a description for a minimalist logo design." With just a little fine-tuning, AI can help you brainstorm ideas or create descriptions that enhance your work.

Similarly, prompt engineering is highly relevant for automation tasks that can make everyday work easier. Imagine you're managing a social media account, and you need to come up with engaging captions for a product launch. Instead of manually brainstorming ideas, you could prompt an AI with something like, "Generate five engaging captions for a new eco-friendly water bottle launch aimed at health-conscious consumers." With a clear and structured prompt, the AI can provide creative suggestions tailored to your specific audience and product, saving you time and effort.

Ultimately, prompt engineering is a skill that anyone can master, regardless of their technical background. It allows individuals to take full advantage of AI's capabilities, whether it's automating tasks, generating content, or solving problems. By learning how to frame prompts effectively, you unlock the power of AI in everyday tasks, making it a valuable tool in both personal and professional settings.

Chapter 2: AI-Powered Personal Branding – Standing Out in the Digital World

Personal branding has evolved dramatically over the past decade, moving far beyond the traditional confines of a well-crafted resume or an impressive LinkedIn profile. In the past, a polished CV or a formal list of accomplishments was often enough to secure job opportunities or establish professional credibility. Today, however, the landscape has changed. The rise of digital platforms, social media, and the interconnectedness of the online world has shifted the focus from static representations of one's experience to dynamic, multifaceted personal brands that can be seen, interacted with, and shared globally.

This evolution is driven by the need for individuals to stand out in an increasingly competitive and digital job market. While resumes and professional profiles still hold value, they no longer tell the whole story. Now, your personal brand is your calling card. It's the collective representation of who you are—your expertise, your voice, your values, and even your personality—spread across various digital platforms. Whether you're a job seeker, an entrepreneur, or a freelancer, how you present yourself online can have a significant impact on how you are perceived by potential employers, clients, and collaborators.

Traditional resumes were often limited to bullet points summarizing work history, education, and skills. These documents were mostly static, only updated when seeking new opportunities. In contrast, a personal brand is a living, evolving entity that reflects not just your past achievements but your ongoing activities, insights, and contributions to your field. It encompasses everything from the content you share on social media to the articles you write, the presentations you give, and the interactions you engage in with others in your industry.

This shift to personal branding is not just about showing what you've done, but about demonstrating what you can do and how you think. People now expect more than just a list of qualifications—they want to see real-world examples of your expertise in action. They want to hear your perspective on industry trends, understand your professional values, and see how you engage with your community. This creates a more holistic and authentic representation of you as a professional.

Moreover, personal branding isn't confined to any particular field. Whether you're in tech, design, healthcare, education, or business, building a strong digital presence is increasingly essential. It allows individuals to differentiate themselves in a crowded marketplace, where traditional resumes might blend into a sea of similar qualifications. A strong personal brand can help you stand out, opening doors to new opportunities, collaborations, and professional networks.

In essence, the evolution from resumes to comprehensive digital personal brands represents a shift from static to dynamic, from a narrow focus on credentials to a broader, more nuanced presentation of one's entire professional self. It empowers individuals to shape how they are perceived by the world, ensuring they can make a lasting impact in today's digital age.

Artificial intelligence has become a powerful tool for personal branding, offering individuals the ability to enhance their digital presence in ways that were once time-consuming or technically complex. AI is now accessible to anyone looking to build a consistent, engaging, and professional personal brand. From designing logos to managing social media accounts and automating content creation, AI tools are streamlining processes and allowing individuals to focus on the creative and strategic aspects of their brand.

One of the most popular ways people leverage AI for personal branding is through logo design.

Traditionally, creating a professional logo required hiring a designer, which could be expensive and time-consuming. Today, AI-driven design tools like Looka or Tailor Brands allow individuals to generate custom logos in a matter of minutes. These platforms analyze user input about their business or personal brand, including style preferences, color schemes, and industry, to create a unique logo that represents their identity. AI ensures that the design process is quick, cost-effective, and accessible, even for those with no design experience.

Social media management is another area where AI is making a significant impact. Maintaining an active and engaging social media presence is essential for personal branding, but it can be overwhelming to consistently post content, respond to comments, and track engagement across multiple platforms. AI-powered tools like Hootsuite, Buffer, and Sprout Social are game-changers in this regard. These platforms use

AI to automate posting schedules, analyze engagement metrics, and even generate content suggestions based on trending topics and user behavior. By using AI, individuals can ensure their social media presence is consistent and engaging without spending hours managing it manually.

AI also plays a crucial role in content creation, a cornerstone of personal branding. Whether it's writing blog posts, crafting social media captions, or generating video scripts, AI-powered tools like Jasper (formerly Jarvis) and Copy.ai assist in producing high-quality content that aligns with an individual's brand message. These tools analyze language patterns, industry keywords, and audience preferences to generate content that feels authentic and relevant. What once took hours of brainstorming and editing can now be done in a fraction of the time, allowing individuals to maintain a steady stream of fresh, consistent content across their platforms.

Consider a freelance graphic designer who recently started using AI tools to elevate her personal brand. Initially, she relied on her portfolio and word-of-mouth referrals to attract clients. However, after integrating an AI-driven design platform to create a sleek, professional logo and using AI tools for content creation, she was able to build a more cohesive and consistent online presence. This helped her stand out in a crowded market, and within months, she saw a noticeable increase in client inquiries and engagement across her social media profiles.

Another example is an entrepreneur who used AI tools to manage his personal brand while launching a new startup. With limited time and resources, he turned to AI-powered social media management platforms to schedule posts, analyze engagement metrics, and ensure his branding remained consistent across multiple channels. By automating routine tasks, he was able to focus on growing his business while maintaining a strong digital presence. AI tools allowed him to interact with his audience in real-time, despite his busy schedule, building trust and credibility with potential investors and customers.

These examples highlight how professionals from various fields—whether freelancing or running a business—can use AI to boost their personal brands. By leveraging AI tools for logo design, content creation, and social media management, they can enhance their visibility and credibility without getting bogged down by the technical details. This enables them to focus on what they do best while letting AI handle the repetitive tasks that ensure a consistent and engaging brand identity.

Chapter 3: Data Storytelling and Visualization – Turning Data into Narrative

Data has become the most valuable resource in the modern world, often referred to as "the new gold." It's the driving force behind many of the technological advancements we see today, from AI-powered decision-making to predictive analytics in business. Organizations and individuals alike are accumulating vast amounts of data, ranging from customer behavior to market trends, medical records, and beyond. This data has the potential to unlock incredible insights, drive innovation, and create competitive advantages. However, like gold in its raw form, data is virtually useless without the ability to extract meaning from it.

The sheer volume of data available today can be overwhelming, and without the ability to process, analyze, and—most importantly—communicate its insights effectively, it becomes nothing more than a collection of numbers. This is where the concept of data storytelling comes into play. Data storytelling is the art of transforming raw data into a compelling narrative that is both insightful and persuasive. It's about taking complex information and presenting it in a way that resonates with people, driving action and influencing decisions.

In a world where data-driven decisions are becoming the norm, the ability to tell stories with data is an invaluable skill. Numbers alone don't inspire change or lead to innovation—it's the human interpretation and communication of those numbers that create real impact. For instance, a company might have access to detailed customer data showing purchasing patterns and preferences. But without the ability to present that data in a clear and engaging way, it's difficult to use it to make informed decisions or to persuade stakeholders to take action.

Data storytelling bridges the gap between cold, hard facts and actionable insights. It allows decision-makers to understand the meaning behind the data, connecting the dots between trends, anomalies, and opportunities. By presenting data in a narrative format, it becomes easier to grasp the broader implications, making it possible to strategize, innovate, and implement solutions that are driven by real-world insights.

For individuals and businesses alike, the true value of data is realized when it's paired with storytelling. Data storytelling makes it possible to turn statistics into a narrative that people can relate to, understand, and act upon. Without this crucial skill, even the most data-rich organizations may find themselves lost in a sea of information, unable to extract meaningful value from the treasure trove of data at their disposal.

AI has revolutionized the way we handle and analyze massive datasets. In today's data-driven world, the amount of information generated every day is staggering—far beyond what any human could manually process. AI algorithms can sift through enormous quantities of data with incredible speed and precision, identifying patterns, trends, and anomalies that would otherwise be difficult or impossible for humans to detect. Whether it's analyzing customer behavior, monitoring market fluctuations, or predicting future trends, AI's ability to process data efficiently is a game-changer for many industries.

However, while AI excels at analyzing data, it still lacks the ability to translate those findings into meaningful, compelling narratives on its own. The human element remains critical in making sense of the data AI processes. AI can deliver insights by revealing trends or correlations, but it takes a human touch to frame those insights within a broader context, making them understandable and actionable. For example, AI might flag a sudden drop in customer engagement, but it's a skilled human analyst who interprets that data, asks the right questions, and presents it in a way that stakeholders can use to make strategic decisions.

Humans bring the intuition, creativity, and empathy needed to turn raw data into a narrative that resonates with others and drives decision-making.

One of the most powerful ways that AI supports data analysis is through data visualization. AI tools are now capable of creating dynamic, interactive visualizations that allow users to explore datasets in ways that would have been impossible with static charts and graphs. Platforms like Tableau, Power BI, and others use AI to generate dashboards that display key data points in a clear and visually engaging format. These visualizations provide a quick and intuitive way to understand complex information, making it easier for decision-makers to grasp the implications of the data at a glance.

In industries like finance, healthcare, retail, and beyond, the ability to visualize data effectively is crucial for decision-making. For instance, in healthcare, AI-driven visualizations can help doctors and administrators track patient outcomes, resource allocation, or the spread of diseases, enabling faster and more informed decisions. In retail, visualizations powered by AI might show how different products are performing in various regions, helping businesses optimize inventory and marketing strategies in real time.

Interactive visualizations also allow users to drill down into the data, exploring specific segments or trends with a click. This makes it easier to uncover hidden insights or answer specific questions that arise during the decision-making process. The combination of AI's data-processing power with human storytelling and the ability to create impactful visualizations results in a highly effective approach to data-driven decision-making. This collaborative dynamic between AI and human interpretation is what makes the data not only accessible but actionable, bridging the gap between numbers and meaningful, real-world outcomes.

Chapter 4: Creative Intelligence Automation – Unlocking Your Creative Potential with AI

The concept of creative intelligence automation represents a powerful fusion of AI technology and human creativity. Rather than replacing the creative instincts and abilities of individuals, AI serves as an enhancer, offering tools and possibilities that can expand the boundaries of what's possible. Creativity has long been thought of as a uniquely human trait—the ability to imagine, innovate, and bring new ideas to life through artistic expression, problem-solving, or invention. However, with the advent of AI, a new era has emerged where machines can support and elevate creative efforts, opening doors to uncharted territories of artistic and intellectual exploration.

Creative intelligence automation refers to the use of AI-driven tools that assist in generating, refining, or experimenting with creative content. Whether it's writing, composing music, designing artwork, or developing new products, AI can automate certain aspects of the creative process, providing inspiration or speeding up workflows. For example, an AI algorithm might help a writer generate ideas for a storyline, suggest melodies for a musician, or propose color schemes for a designer. The machine provides possibilities, but it's the human who makes the critical decisions, adding their unique touch and vision.

What makes this collaboration between AI and human creativity so compelling is that it allows for experimentation that might not have been possible otherwise. AI can analyze vast amounts of existing data or past creative works to suggest new combinations, patterns, or approaches that a human might not have considered. A graphic designer, for instance, can use AI to generate hundreds of variations of a design concept in seconds, exploring a wide array of possibilities before choosing the one that resonates the most.

This ability to quickly iterate on ideas expands the creative process, allowing humans to focus more on the refinement and personalization of their work rather than starting from scratch every time.

Far from limiting creativity, AI can also introduce entirely new genres or styles that wouldn't have existed without machine assistance. For example, musicians can use AI to experiment with new soundscapes or genres that fuse different musical elements in ways that transcend traditional styles. In art, AI-generated visuals can inspire new forms of expression that blend the abstract and the real, pushing the boundaries of contemporary art. While AI contributes to these outputs, the true artistry comes from the human's ability to guide the process, make choices, and infuse it with meaning and emotion.

The key to understanding creative intelligence automation is recognizing that AI does not replace the human role in creativity—it amplifies it. By automating the more time-consuming or repetitive aspects of the creative process, AI allows individuals to focus on what they do best: making creative decisions, innovating, and adding personal expression to their work. Rather than seeing AI as a threat to creativity, it should be viewed as a tool that enhances the possibilities, making room for even greater human ingenuity and artistic achievement.

In this sense, AI becomes a collaborator in the creative process, offering new avenues for exploration while leaving the core of human creativity intact. The result is a powerful partnership between technology and the human mind, where AI-driven automation accelerates and enhances creativity, allowing humans to push the limits of what's possible in their art, music, writing, and beyond.

Artificial intelligence is transforming creative fields such as music, design, and art, pushing the boundaries of innovation in ways that were once unimaginable. In music, AI has the ability to compose original pieces by analyzing existing patterns and styles from vast databases of songs. Tools like Amper Music and AIVA (Artificial Intelligence Virtual Artist) allow musicians to collaborate with AI to generate melodies, harmonies, and even entire compositions. These AI tools can take into account user input such as genre, tempo, and mood to create custom tracks that musicians can then refine and personalize. Instead of replacing musicians, AI acts as a creative assistant, helping them experiment with new ideas and generate content quickly.

In the realm of design, AI-driven platforms such as Canva and Adobe Sensei have revolutionized graphic design, offering features that help designers create professional-quality visuals in a fraction of the time. AI tools can analyze trends, suggest layouts, and even generate logo designs, freeing up designers to focus on the more conceptual aspects of their work. For example, AI can automatically balance color schemes, adjust spacing, or recommend font pairings that would otherwise require manual adjustment. This allows designers to experiment with numerous variations of their designs without getting bogged down by technical details, making the creative process more fluid and expansive.

In the world of art, AI-generated visuals are pushing the boundaries of traditional artistic expression. Artists are using AI algorithms to create entirely new forms of digital art, blending abstraction with real-world imagery to produce works that challenge conventional styles. One well-known example is the use of Generative Adversarial Networks (GANs), which can create intricate, dreamlike images by learning from thousands of visual inputs. AI-driven art tools like DeepDream and Runway ML allow artists to merge their own creative vision with AI's ability to manipulate pixels, colors, and patterns in ways that stretch the imagination. The result is often a collaboration between human intuition and machine intelligence, creating pieces that blur the line between what's human-made and machine-assisted.

Beyond individual art forms, AI's impact on creativity is only limited by one's willingness to experiment with it. The possibilities AI offers are truly limitless for those open to pushing the boundaries of their craft. In film and video production, for instance, AI tools can assist in editing, color grading, and even generating entire visual effects. In writing, AI platforms such as GPT-4 can help authors brainstorm, draft, or revise content, allowing them to focus more on the flow of ideas rather than the mechanics of writing.

The key to unlocking AI's creative potential lies in embracing experimentation. Artists, musicians, and creators who are willing to explore these tools can break free from traditional constraints and discover new methods of expression. By leveraging AI's ability to process massive amounts of data and generate fresh insights, creators are no longer bound by the limitations of manual effort or time-consuming processes. Instead, they can collaborate with AI to explore new genres, styles, and mediums, resulting in innovative works that push the boundaries of their respective fields.

For those who dare to experiment, AI opens doors to creative exploration that have no boundaries. Whether it's blending genres in music, merging digital and physical art forms, or using AI to create entirely new design concepts, the potential is vast. The future of creativity lies not in seeing AI as a replacement for human talent but as a tool that expands what's possible, enabling creators to achieve more, faster, and with greater innovation. By tapping into this limitless potential, the world of art, music, and design is set to undergo a radical transformation, one where the fusion of human creativity and AI's capabilities will redefine what it means to create.

Chapter 5: AI Strategy and Execution – The Key to Business Success

Artificial intelligence has rapidly become a critical component of modern business strategies, reshaping how companies operate across virtually every industry. From automating routine tasks to driving innovative decision-making, AI is helping businesses increase efficiency, improve customer experiences, and gain a competitive edge. The integration of AI is no longer limited to large tech companies; businesses of all sizes and sectors are incorporating AI into their daily operations to streamline processes and maximize productivity.

In the retail sector, AI is being used to enhance customer experiences through personalized recommendations and automated customer service. E-commerce platforms like Amazon and Shopify use AI algorithms to analyze customers' browsing and purchase histories, generating tailored product recommendations that increase sales and customer satisfaction. Chatbots powered by natural language processing (NLP) handle customer inquiries, offering real-time support that reduces the need for human intervention, while predictive analytics helps retailers anticipate demand and optimize inventory management.

Manufacturing industries have embraced AI to revolutionize production processes. AI-driven systems can monitor and control machinery, reducing human error and ensuring optimal performance. Predictive maintenance powered by AI analyzes equipment data to forecast potential failures, allowing companies to perform maintenance before costly breakdowns occur. This not only reduces downtime but also extends the lifespan of machinery, leading to significant cost savings. Moreover, AI-driven robotics have transformed assembly lines, improving precision and speed in manufacturing operations.

In the finance sector, AI is transforming how institutions manage risk, detect fraud, and make investment decisions. Banks and financial firms are using machine learning algorithms to analyze large datasets and identify suspicious transactions in real-time, enhancing security and compliance efforts. AI-powered financial advisors or robo-advisors provide personalized investment recommendations by analyzing market trends and individual client preferences, offering services that were once limited to high-net-worth individuals. Furthermore, AI models help in credit scoring, assessing the risk of lending to customers more accurately than traditional methods.

Healthcare has seen a surge in AI applications that are transforming patient care, diagnostics, and research. AI algorithms can analyze medical images, such as X-rays and MRIs, with remarkable accuracy, assisting doctors in early diagnosis of conditions like cancer. AI-driven predictive models help in assessing patient risk factors, enabling personalized treatment plans that improve outcomes. Additionally, AI-powered virtual health assistants and chatbots are being used to manage appointments, answer health-related queries, and provide patients with important reminders, streamlining administrative processes.

The logistics and supply chain industry has also benefited greatly from AI integration. AI tools optimize routes for delivery trucks, reducing fuel consumption and improving delivery times. Machine learning algorithms analyze data from global supply chains, helping companies anticipate disruptions, identify inefficiencies, and manage inventory more effectively. By automating these processes, businesses can reduce costs, improve service levels, and adapt more quickly to changing market conditions.

In marketing, AI is being utilized to target advertising campaigns more precisely and analyze consumer behavior with greater depth. Companies use AI-powered tools to personalize marketing messages, optimizing the timing and content of advertisements based on individual preferences and behaviors. AI-driven analytics provide insights into campaign performance, allowing marketers to make data-driven adjustments in real-time to maximize engagement and return on investment.

Across industries, businesses are also integrating AI into human resources and recruitment processes. AI tools can scan resumes, analyze job applications, and even conduct initial interviews, identifying the best candidates for open positions. This automation reduces the time spent on hiring while ensuring that decisions are based on data rather than human biases. In addition, AI is being used to assess employee performance, predict turnover, and recommend personalized development plans, creating a more data-driven approach to talent management.

The widespread integration of AI into business operations has created opportunities for companies to enhance efficiency, improve customer satisfaction, and drive innovation. Whether through automating repetitive tasks, optimizing complex processes, or offering personalized services, AI is reshaping the future of business across all sectors. The companies that embrace AI are better positioned to thrive in an increasingly competitive and data-driven economy.

To fully harness the power of artificial intelligence, businesses must develop a clear and focused AI strategy that aligns with their overall goals. AI should not be implemented for the sake of novelty; rather, it needs to be integrated thoughtfully, ensuring that it addresses specific business challenges or opportunities. Companies that succeed with AI are those that carefully consider how the technology fits within their larger objectives, ensuring that it serves a functional purpose while enhancing operations.

A critical first step in building a clear AI strategy is to identify key areas where AI can deliver measurable value. This requires a thorough analysis of current business processes to understand where AI can optimize efficiency, reduce costs, or improve customer experiences. For example, a company might identify that their customer service operations are struggling to keep up with demand. In this case, AI-driven chatbots or virtual assistants could be introduced to handle routine inquiries, freeing up human agents to focus on more complex or high-value tasks. By identifying these pressure points, businesses can focus their AI efforts on areas that will yield the highest return.

Next, it's important to set clear, measurable goals for AI implementation. Companies should define success criteria, whether it's a reduction in processing times, an increase in customer satisfaction, or improved accuracy in predictions. Having clear objectives allows businesses to track the effectiveness of their AI initiatives and make adjustments as necessary. For example, if the goal is to improve the accuracy of demand forecasting, the company should track key metrics such as forecasting accuracy and inventory levels over time, ensuring that the AI tools are delivering tangible results.

Another essential aspect of an AI strategy is ensuring that the technology integrates seamlessly with existing systems and workflows. Many AI tools require access to large datasets to function effectively, so companies need to ensure that their data infrastructure is robust and capable of supporting these systems. This may involve upgrading current databases, enhancing cybersecurity measures to protect sensitive information, or investing in cloud-based solutions that enable real-time data processing. Ensuring data quality and accessibility is a key factor in maximizing the benefits of AI.

Finally, companies must foster a culture of continuous learning and adaptability. AI is an ever-evolving field, and to stay ahead, businesses need to remain open to experimentation and innovation. This means not only training employees to work alongside AI but also staying up to date with the latest advancements in the technology. Encouraging collaboration between AI specialists, data scientists, and business leaders ensures that AI tools are used to their full potential and that any challenges can be addressed collectively.

In retail, companies like Walmart have successfully integrated AI to improve their supply chain and inventory management. Walmart uses AI-powered tools to predict customer demand more accurately, ensuring that popular items are always in stock while reducing waste from overstocking. By analyzing past purchase data and external factors such as weather patterns, AI systems can forecast trends and adjust inventory levels in real-time. This has not only improved efficiency but also significantly reduced costs.

In the marketing sector, Coca-Cola has embraced AI to personalize its advertising campaigns. The company uses AI-driven analytics to analyze consumer data, identifying patterns and preferences that help shape targeted marketing efforts. For example, Coca-Cola's AI tools help create personalized social media content and targeted advertisements based on real-time consumer behavior. This tailored approach has helped the brand engage more meaningfully with its audience, increasing both brand loyalty and sales.

In customer service, companies like Delta Airlines have implemented AI-powered virtual assistants to improve the customer experience. Delta's AI-driven chatbot, integrated into their mobile app, helps customers check flight statuses, book flights, and resolve issues without needing to contact a human agent. This has significantly reduced wait times for customers and allowed the airline to provide faster, more efficient service. By automating routine tasks, Delta's human customer service agents can focus on resolving more complex issues, improving overall satisfaction.

These examples highlight how a clear, well aligned AI strategy can benefit businesses across various sectors. Whether it's optimizing operations, improving customer engagement, or enhancing decision-making, AI can drive measurable results when implemented with purpose and precision. By identifying key areas for AI application, setting clear goals, ensuring seamless integration, and fostering a culture of innovation, companies can ensure that AI serves as a powerful tool for growth and success.

Chapter 6: AI Project Management – Overseeing the Future of Innovation

Managing AI projects presents unique challenges that require a blend of both technical and non-technical skills. Unlike traditional projects, where goals and deliverables might be more clearly defined, AI projects often involve working with evolving technologies, complex datasets, and systems that require ongoing refinement. This complexity means that AI project managers must not only have a strong grasp of the technical aspects of AI systems but also the ability to navigate the broader organizational and strategic implications that come with implementing such technologies.

One of the main technical challenges in AI project management is understanding how AI models work and ensuring they are being developed and deployed effectively. AI project managers need to have a foundational knowledge of machine learning, natural language processing, or other relevant AI technologies to communicate effectively with data scientists and developers. They must understand the basics of how AI algorithms are trained, how data influences the model, and what limitations may arise from the underlying technology. Even if they are not building the models themselves, project managers must be able to ask the right questions, identify potential technical roadblocks, and ensure that the project stays on track from a development standpoint.

However, being technically proficient alone is not enough. AI project managers must also excel in non-technical skills, such as communication, leadership, and problem-solving. AI projects often involve cross-functional teams that include data scientists, software engineers, business stakeholders, and end-users. The project manager needs to bridge the gap between these different groups, ensuring that everyone is aligned with the project's objectives. This requires the ability to translate technical jargon into language that non-technical team members can understand, and vice versa, ensuring that business goals are reflected in the technical execution.

Additionally, one of the biggest non-technical challenges in AI project management is managing stakeholder expectations. AI is often seen as a magical solution that will instantly solve complex problems or automate entire processes. It is the project manager's role to set realistic expectations and communicate the limitations of AI systems clearly. Not all AI models will produce perfect results immediately, and many require continuous training and adjustment. AI project managers must convey this to stakeholders to avoid disappointment and ensure that the project stays aligned with business goals over the long term.

Risk management is another key area where both technical and non-technical skills intersect. AI projects often involve dealing with large amounts of data, some of which may be sensitive or regulated. The project manager must ensure that data privacy laws, such as GDPR, are adhered to, and that the data being used is accurate and properly managed. Additionally, AI models can sometimes produce biased or inaccurate outcomes, so project managers need to have contingency plans in place and ensure that ethical considerations are part of the development process.

The iterative nature of AI development also presents unique challenges. Unlike many other types of projects where there is a clear endpoint, AI projects often require continuous improvement and adaptation. Models need to be regularly updated as new data becomes available or as business needs change. Managing these ongoing adjustments requires flexibility and adaptability, as well as the ability to keep the project within budget and on schedule despite these constant changes.

AI project managers must also excel in managing team dynamics. AI projects often involve highly specialized talent, such as data scientists and AI researchers, who may have different working styles and needs compared to traditional software developers. Ensuring that the team collaborates effectively, stays motivated, and works towards a common goal is critical to the project's success.

In summary, AI project management requires a unique combination of technical knowledge and soft skills. AI project managers must not only understand the technical details of how AI systems are built and maintained but also navigate the complexities of organizational alignment, stakeholder management, risk mitigation, and team leadership. Balancing these technical and non-technical challenges ensures that AI projects are delivered successfully and provide real value to the organization.

Successfully managing AI projects requires clear objectives, effective risk management, and strong communication skills to ensure that both technical and business goals are met. AI projects often differ from traditional IT projects due to their complexity, reliance on data, and the iterative nature of development. Understanding the key elements that drive the success of AI projects is crucial for project managers who must navigate a combination of technical challenges and stakeholder expectations.

The first and most essential step in managing AI projects is setting clear, measurable objectives. Unlike traditional projects where the deliverables may be more straightforward, AI projects often involve creating systems that will evolve over time, and their success can be subjective. To mitigate this, project managers need to work closely with stakeholders to define what success looks like early in the project. For example, if the project involves developing an AI-powered recommendation engine, the objectives should specify metrics such as increased customer engagement, higher sales conversions, or improved user satisfaction. These objectives should be quantifiable and aligned with the organization's broader business goals. Defining key performance indicators (KPIs) that track the AI system's performance is critical in evaluating its success over time.

Risk management is another vital element in overseeing AI projects. AI systems, by nature, rely on large datasets and complex algorithms, which introduces several layers of risk. One major risk is the potential for biased data or inaccurate outcomes. Project managers must ensure that the data being used to train AI models is representative and unbiased, as biased training data can result in skewed predictions or decisions. To manage this risk, the project team should establish checks and validation procedures to monitor for biases throughout development. Ethical considerations, such as data privacy and the potential for unintended harm, must also be factored into the risk management process. Moreover, AI models are often unpredictable, meaning that they may not perform as expected in certain scenarios, and contingency plans should be in place to address such uncertainties.

Communication is at the heart of successful AI project management. Given the technical complexity of AI systems, project managers must act as a bridge between the technical teams, such as data scientists and engineers, and business stakeholders. This requires the ability to translate technical findings into actionable insights that stakeholders can understand. For instance, if an AI model is underperforming or requires further training, project managers need to explain why this is happening and what steps are being taken to improve the system. Clear, ongoing communication ensures that stakeholders remain informed about progress, risks, and any changes to the project scope. Regular updates, including status reports and presentations, should be part of the communication plan to keep everyone aligned.

One real-world scenario that illustrates the complexities of AI project management is the deployment of an AI-powered chatbot for a large corporation. Let's imagine a company that wants to use AI to handle customer service inquiries more efficiently. The objective is to create a chatbot that can answer frequently asked questions, resolve common issues, and direct customers to human agents when necessary. The project manager's role in this scenario involves several key responsibilities.

First, the project manager must work with both the business team and technical team to define clear objectives for the chatbot. For example, the success criteria might include metrics such as reducing the average response time by 50%, handling 70% of customer queries without human intervention, and maintaining a 90% customer satisfaction rate. These objectives help guide the development process and provide measurable goals to assess the chatbot's effectiveness once it's live.

Next, managing the risks associated with the deployment of the chatbot is critical. One significant risk could be the chatbot misunderstanding user inputs, leading to customer frustration. To mitigate this, the project manager would work with data scientists to ensure that the chatbot's natural language processing (NLP) capabilities are well-trained on a comprehensive dataset that includes diverse customer inquiries. Additionally, the project manager might establish fallback mechanisms, such as ensuring that the chatbot can seamlessly transfer users to human agents when it encounters a question it cannot answer. Monitoring real-time interactions post-launch to refine the chatbot's responses is also essential in managing long-term risk.

Effective communication plays a key role in the success of this project. The project manager needs to continuously update business leaders on the chatbot's progress, provide insights into any challenges (such as delays in training the AI model), and keep the technical team aligned with the business goals. For example, if customer feedback suggests that the chatbot is not responding appropriately to certain types of questions, the project manager must relay this information to the development team and adjust the project plan to address these issues.

In another example, consider a retail company implementing AI to predict customer demand and optimize inventory management. The project manager's objective is to ensure that the AI system provides accurate demand forecasts, reducing overstock and stockout situations by 30%. The project team needs to train the AI model on historical sales data, incorporating factors such as seasonality, promotions, and regional preferences. Managing the risk of inaccurate forecasts involves thorough data validation and regular model performance testing. Clear communication with inventory managers and the sales team ensures that the AI system is being fine-tuned based on real-world feedback.

In both cases, the combination of setting clear objectives, managing risks, and maintaining transparent communication is essential for delivering successful AI projects. These elements allow project managers to navigate the technical complexities of AI while ensuring that the projects deliver real value to the business.

Chapter 7: Natural Language Processing (NLP) – The Language of AI

Natural Language Processing (NLP) is a branch of artificial intelligence that focuses on the interaction between computers and humans through natural language. In simple terms, NLP enables AI systems to understand, interpret, and respond to human language in a way that feels natural and intuitive. This capability is essential for making AI systems more accessible, as it allows machines to communicate in human terms rather than requiring users to interact with complex code or specific commands. NLP bridges the gap between human communication and machine understanding, making it a critical component of many AI applications today.

The importance of NLP lies in its ability to break down and process human language, which is often messy, ambiguous, and context-dependent. Human language is filled with nuances such as idioms, slang, and varying tones, making it difficult for computers to interpret without sophisticated processing techniques. NLP allows AI systems to handle these complexities by analyzing the structure of sentences, identifying key words and phrases, and understanding the context in which they are used. This enables AI to grasp the meaning behind a user's input and generate responses that are relevant and accurate.

NLP plays a key role in many of the AI-powered tools we use daily, from voice assistants like Siri and Alexa to chatbots that provide customer support. When you ask a virtual assistant to set a reminder or search for information, it's NLP that interprets your spoken command, determines what you're asking, and executes the task. Similarly, in customer service applications, NLP enables chatbots to understand and respond to user queries, making it possible for businesses to offer real-time support without the need for human intervention.

Another critical aspect of NLP is its ability to analyze large amounts of text data. Businesses use NLP to analyze customer feedback, social media posts, and product reviews, gaining valuable insights into customer preferences and sentiments. By processing text at scale, NLP helps companies make data-driven decisions based on how customers are feeling or reacting to a particular product, service, or campaign. This ability to analyze and interpret language data is transforming industries by enabling more personalized, responsive, and effective customer engagement.

The ultimate goal of NLP is to make AI systems more human-like in their communication, allowing them to understand and generate language that is coherent and contextually appropriate. This makes it easier for people to interact with AI in natural and intuitive ways, whether they're asking a simple question, having a conversation, or requesting specific actions. As AI systems become more adept at understanding human language, they also become more useful in a wide range of applications, from healthcare to education, entertainment, and beyond.

In essence, NLP is a crucial technology that enables AI to engage with humans on their terms, making interactions with machines feel more natural, efficient, and accessible. By mastering the complexities of language, NLP allows AI to better understand our needs and respond in ways that enhance our daily lives.

Natural Language Processing (NLP) has become an integral part of many industries, driving efficiencies and improving how businesses interact with customers and manage communication. In practical terms, NLP allows AI systems to comprehend, interpret, and respond to human language in ways that were once impossible. Its application in customer service has been particularly transformative, where NLP is used in chatbots and virtual assistants to handle routine inquiries and provide real-time support. Businesses leverage

NLP-powered chatbots to resolve common issues, answer questions, and even process transactions without needing human intervention. These systems not only enhance response times but also reduce operational costs by allowing human agents to focus on more complex problems. As a result, customer satisfaction improves while businesses maintain efficiency at scale.

In the realm of social media, NLP plays a crucial role in monitoring brand reputation and sentiment analysis. With millions of posts, comments, and messages generated every day, businesses rely on AI to process this vast amount of text and derive insights. NLP systems can detect positive or negative sentiment from customer feedback, analyze trending topics, and even predict potential issues before they escalate. For example, a company can track how a product launch is being received on social media platforms by analyzing the language used by customers in their posts. If sentiment turns negative, businesses can respond quickly with appropriate solutions or adjustments to their messaging. This ability to understand real-time public perception provides businesses with a competitive edge, allowing them to remain agile and responsive to their audience's needs.

Beyond customer service and social media, NLP has applications in content generation, data extraction, and personalized marketing. AI-powered tools can create tailored content such as product descriptions, email campaigns, or even blog posts based on specific inputs and audience preferences. For instance, an e-commerce platform might use NLP to automatically generate engaging product descriptions based on user-generated data and keywords. Similarly, businesses can personalize their marketing messages by analyzing customer interactions and preferences, ensuring that communications are both relevant and timely. This allows for more targeted campaigns, improving engagement and conversion rates.

NLP is also being used in fields like healthcare, where it can help analyze patient records, transcribe doctor-patient conversations, and assist in diagnosing conditions based on symptoms described in natural language. This not only speeds up administrative tasks but also supports healthcare providers in making better-informed decisions. NLP tools can extract relevant information from unstructured data such as medical notes and provide insights that enhance patient care.

As NLP continues to evolve, its ability to shape communication across industries is becoming even more apparent. By enabling AI systems to interpret human language with greater accuracy and context, NLP is revolutionizing how businesses respond to both internal and external communications. One of the key ways it's doing this is by improving the quality of automated responses. AI is no longer restricted to answering basic queries with generic replies. Instead, it can understand the nuances of language, detect underlying emotions, and provide contextually appropriate responses. This allows businesses to engage with customers in a more meaningful and human-like manner, making AI interactions feel more personalized.

In marketing, NLP helps companies craft more effective strategies by analyzing consumer behavior and preferences. Through the interpretation of language used in customer feedback, online reviews, and social media, NLP can identify patterns and trends that inform product development, promotional tactics, and customer engagement efforts. The ability to analyze vast amounts of data quickly and accurately ensures that businesses are not only reactive but also proactive in addressing consumer needs.

In sectors like education and legal services, NLP is streamlining processes by automating text analysis and document management. In education, AI-driven tutoring systems can evaluate written responses, offer personalized feedback, and guide students through learning materials based on their language use and comprehension. In legal services, NLP helps attorneys analyze large volumes of legal texts, contracts, and case law, making research faster and more precise.

Ultimately, NLP is revolutionizing industries by enabling AI to interpret human language more effectively, leading to better responses and strategies. By allowing businesses to understand and respond to customer needs in real-time, automate routine tasks, and make data-driven decisions, NLP is transforming communication and making AI a more powerful tool for business growth.

Chapter 8: Continuous Learning and Curiosity – The Mindset of AI Leaders

The rapid evolution of artificial intelligence has made it one of the most dynamic fields in technology today. Every day, new breakthroughs, tools, and applications emerge, reshaping industries and pushing the boundaries of what is possible. In this ever-changing landscape, the ability to stay curious and commit to continuous learning is not just a recommendation—it's a necessity. For professionals who want to remain competitive and relevant, adaptability and a mindset of lifelong learning are crucial to navigating the swift pace of AI advancements.

AI is evolving at such a speed that skills learned just a few years ago may quickly become outdated. What was once cutting-edge, like basic machine learning models or early versions of natural language processing, has now been replaced by more sophisticated technologies like deep learning algorithms and advanced AI-powered systems capable of tasks that were once considered purely science fiction. As these advancements continue, keeping up with the latest tools and techniques requires a willingness to dive into new areas and explore unfamiliar concepts.

Staying curious fuels this journey. A curious mind is always on the lookout for new possibilities, eager to experiment with emerging technologies and unafraid to challenge the status quo. Curiosity drives individuals to ask questions, explore different perspectives, and embrace the unknown—traits that are essential in a field like AI, where constant innovation and disruption are the norm. By maintaining a natural curiosity, professionals can stay ahead of the curve, spotting trends before they become mainstream and experimenting with AI solutions that offer transformative potential.

Continuous learning is equally important, as AI demands both theoretical knowledge and hands-on experience. Whether through formal education, online courses, or self-driven projects, dedicating time to learn new AI frameworks, algorithms, or programming languages is essential. It's not enough to rely on past knowledge; the field's ongoing advancements require practitioners to refresh their skills regularly. Additionally, AI is an interdisciplinary field, intersecting with areas like data science, ethics, robotics, and cognitive psychology. This means that learning isn't confined to AI alone—broadening one's understanding of related areas can enhance problem-solving and innovation within AI.

For instance, those working with AI might start by mastering foundational technologies like Python programming and machine learning algorithms. However, as new frameworks or AI tools like TensorFlow, PyTorch, or OpenAI become more prevalent, staying up-to-date ensures that these professionals remain capable of handling the most current projects. Likewise, continuous learning encourages experimentation with new applications of AI, whether it's integrating AI into healthcare, developing autonomous vehicles, or using AI for creative arts.

The fast-paced nature of AI also brings challenges that require ongoing problem-solving and adaptability. As AI systems become more advanced, so do the ethical concerns, technical obstacles, and social implications that come with them. Being open to learning not just about the technologies themselves but also about how they interact with broader societal issues is critical. Ethical AI development, for instance, is an area that demands constant reflection and learning, as the impact of AI on privacy, bias, and fairness becomes more pronounced.

For businesses, staying curious and fostering a culture of continuous learning are crucial for driving innovation. Companies that invest in their teams' development and encourage them to explore new AI tools or methods are better positioned to capitalize on the benefits AI offers. It also allows organizations to be more agile, pivoting quickly as new AI trends emerge or as industry needs shift. By keeping up with the latest AI trends and educating themselves on emerging tools, businesses can ensure they remain competitive in a marketplace where technological expertise is increasingly becoming a key differentiator.

In conclusion, the fast-paced evolution of AI demands both curiosity and a commitment to lifelong learning. The ability to adapt, explore, and grow with the technology is what separates those who merely use AI from those who master it. In this dynamic field, the curiosity to question and the willingness to learn are the keys to staying relevant, pushing boundaries, and unlocking the full potential of artificial intelligence.

Being a lifelong learner in the field of artificial intelligence is not only about staying informed but also about continuously evolving and adapting to the fast-changing landscape. Maintaining a learning mindset requires dedication, curiosity, and a proactive approach to acquiring new knowledge and skills. There are several practical strategies to cultivate this mindset, including taking courses, experimenting with emerging technologies, and engaging in self-driven projects.

One of the most accessible ways to maintain a learning mindset is through online courses. Platforms like Coursera, Udemy, and edX offer a wide range of AI-focused courses that cover everything from the basics of machine learning to advanced deep learning techniques. These courses are often taught by experts in the field, providing learners with up-to-date information and real-world applications of AI. By consistently enrolling in these courses, professionals can keep their skills sharp and remain aware of new trends, tools, and methodologies. Many of these platforms also offer certifications, which can be a valuable way to demonstrate mastery in specific AI disciplines.

Experimentation is another powerful way to maintain a learning mindset. AI is a field that thrives on hands-on experience, and there is no better way to understand new concepts than by experimenting with them. Tools like TensorFlow, PyTorch, and OpenAI's API are freely available for anyone to explore. Setting up personal projects that involve building simple AI models, creating chatbots, or experimenting with data analysis using machine learning algorithms can solidify one's understanding of the core principles while fostering creativity and problem-solving skills. By engaging with these tools and working through challenges, professionals can develop a deeper intuition for how AI systems work.

Self-driven projects are particularly effective because they allow individuals to tailor their learning to areas of interest or emerging trends. For instance, someone interested in natural language processing (NLP) might start a project that involves training a language model to generate human-like text, while a person focused on computer vision might build a model that recognizes objects in images. These projects not only help build technical skills but also foster innovation by encouraging learners to push the boundaries of what they know. Importantly, they also provide portfolio material that can showcase one's capabilities to potential employers or collaborators.

Conferences, workshops, and hackathons also play a crucial role in maintaining a learning mindset. Events like the Neural Information Processing Systems (NeurIPS) conference or workshops hosted by tech companies are excellent opportunities to engage with the latest research, meet experts, and collaborate with peers. Hackathons, in particular, offer a competitive but collaborative environment where participants can apply their skills to solve real-world problems in a short amount of time, accelerating learning and providing exposure to new technologies.

Books and research papers are another key resource for those dedicated to lifelong learning. Reading books by AI pioneers such as *Deep Learning* by Ian Goodfellow or *Artificial Intelligence: A Modern Approach* by Stuart Russell and Peter Norvig can provide foundational knowledge, while keeping up with research papers from platforms like arXiv.org ensures that professionals are aware of cutting-edge developments. Staying informed through these resources helps learners build a broad understanding of AI while also diving deep into specific areas of interest.

For those who adopt a lifelong learning approach, the benefits go far beyond personal development. It allows professionals to stay ahead of the curve, positioning themselves as leaders in a rapidly evolving field. Take, for example, Andrew Ng, a prominent figure in AI and co-founder of Coursera. Ng has remained a leading voice in AI education by continuously exploring new AI applications, from his early work on deep learning at Google Brain to his current efforts in AI for healthcare and industries beyond tech. His commitment to learning and teaching has enabled him to stay relevant and influential as the field of AI has grown.

Another example is Fei-Fei Li, a pioneering AI researcher in computer vision and co-director of Stanford's Human-Centered AI Institute. Li has maintained her relevance not just by contributing to groundbreaking research but also by advocating for the ethical development of AI and its applications in areas such as healthcare and education. Her continuous learning and adaptability have allowed her to remain at the forefront of AI innovation while addressing the social implications of the technology.

Similarly, individuals who are dedicated to learning have seen significant benefits in the business world. Take Elon Musk's Tesla, for instance. Tesla's AI-driven self-driving technology is the result of a company-wide commitment to experimentation, continuous learning, and innovation. Tesla's engineers and AI researchers have consistently stayed ahead by exploring new technologies and refining their systems through real-world data and testing. This dedication to evolving alongside AI advancements has enabled Tesla to maintain its leadership in the electric vehicle and autonomous driving space.

In essence, maintaining a learning mindset is about consistently pushing boundaries, staying curious, and being open to new ideas. By taking courses, experimenting with projects, attending events, and continuously engaging with the AI community, professionals can ensure they stay ahead in a field that is evolving at an unprecedented pace. Those who commit to lifelong learning in AI are not just keeping up—they are leading the way, driving innovation, and shaping the future of the technology.

Chapter 9: Understanding AI Limitations – Navigating Pitfalls and Risks

Artificial intelligence has the power to transform industries and redefine the way we live and work. Its ability to process vast amounts of data, identify patterns, and make predictions at incredible speeds has made AI an essential tool in many areas. However, despite its impressive capabilities, AI is not without its flaws. Understanding these limitations is crucial for managing expectations and ensuring responsible use. Among the most significant concerns are the risks of bias, errors, and the necessity of human oversight to ensure AI systems function ethically and effectively.

One of the most well-known limitations of AI is the risk of bias in its outputs. AI systems learn from the data they are trained on, and if that data contains biased information, the AI can replicate and even exacerbate those biases. For example, if an AI model used for hiring decisions is trained on historical data that reflects gender or racial biases, it may perpetuate those biases by unfairly favoring certain groups over others. This has already been observed in AI-driven recruitment systems, where certain demographics were underrepresented or misjudged based on biased data inputs. Bias in AI extends beyond hiring; it can affect areas like criminal justice, healthcare, and lending, where biased decisions can have serious consequences.

Another challenge with AI is its propensity for errors, particularly when the data it processes is incomplete, incorrect, or poorly structured. AI models depend on the quality of the data they are fed, and inaccuracies in the input data can lead to faulty conclusions or predictions. For example, in the medical field, an AI system designed to diagnose diseases may misidentify symptoms if the training data lacks comprehensive representation of different patient groups or conditions. Similarly, in financial markets, AI algorithms may make poor investment decisions if they fail to account for unforeseen external factors or if they rely too heavily on historical data that no longer applies to current market conditions. While AI can be remarkably accurate when provided with high-quality data, it is not immune to mistakes.

Moreover, AI systems often operate as "black boxes," meaning that the decision-making process is not always transparent. Even the engineers and developers who create these systems may struggle to fully understand how the AI arrived at a particular conclusion. This lack of explainability is particularly problematic in fields where accountability is critical, such as healthcare or law enforcement. If an AI system makes an incorrect or unfair decision, it can be difficult to pinpoint the cause or to rectify the problem. This opacity underscores the need for human oversight to ensure that AI systems are being used appropriately and to intervene when things go wrong.

Human oversight is essential not only to mitigate bias and correct errors but also to apply ethical considerations that AI systems inherently lack. AI, by nature, is purely data-driven and operates without moral or ethical reasoning. It can analyze patterns and make predictions, but it lacks the capacity for empathy, judgment, or understanding of broader societal impacts. For example, an AI system might recommend a course of action that is efficient and logical from a purely data-centric perspective but could be harmful or unfair from an ethical standpoint. In healthcare, an AI might suggest prioritizing certain treatments based on statistical probabilities, but human doctors are needed to consider the nuances of patient care, such as personal preferences or unique circumstances that the AI cannot account for.

Additionally, AI systems can sometimes struggle with handling edge cases—scenarios that fall outside the norm or are too complex for the model to process. While AI excels at identifying patterns in large datasets, it may falter when faced with highly specific, atypical situations that require contextual understanding or creative problem-solving. For instance, a self-driving car might navigate most environments flawlessly but could struggle in an unfamiliar or unpredictable situation, such as a construction site with unclear road markings. In these instances, human intervention is critical to ensure safety and appropriate decision-making.

The limitations of AI also highlight the need for ongoing human involvement in its development and deployment. AI systems require continuous monitoring, testing, and refinement to ensure they are functioning as intended and adapting to changing conditions. This iterative process demands collaboration between AI engineers, data scientists, and domain experts who can provide context and expertise that AI lacks. It's not enough to simply build an AI system and set it loose—constant evaluation is necessary to address its shortcomings and prevent potential harm.

Ultimately, while AI offers incredible potential, it is far from perfect. Bias, errors, and the need for human oversight are significant challenges that must be addressed to ensure AI is used responsibly and ethically. The power of AI lies in its ability to enhance human capabilities, not replace them. By understanding AI's limitations and applying careful oversight, we can harness its potential while minimizing its risks, ensuring that AI serves as a tool for positive, equitable outcomes rather than perpetuating inequalities or creating new problems.

There are numerous scenarios where AI systems, despite their potential, might make flawed decisions due to poor data quality or inherent biases embedded in the models. Understanding when not to trust AI is critical in fields where the consequences of errors can be significant, such as healthcare, criminal justice, finance, and even everyday business operations. AI, after all, is only as reliable as the data it is trained on and the context in which it is used.

One common scenario where AI might make flawed decisions is when the data used to train the model is biased, incomplete, or not representative of the broader population. For example, in hiring processes, if an AI model is trained on historical data from a company that has traditionally hired predominantly one demographic, the AI might learn to favor applicants from that same demographic, perpetuating a cycle of bias. Similarly, facial recognition technologies have been shown to perform poorly on certain racial and ethnic groups because they were trained on datasets that lacked diversity. In these cases, the AI system's decisions can reinforce existing inequalities rather than providing fair and objective assessments.

AI systems also struggle in situations where they encounter edge cases or unusual scenarios that they were not trained to handle. For instance, in self-driving cars, AI may perform well in predictable environments but could fail to react appropriately in complex, dynamic situations like construction zones or emergency conditions. Because AI lacks the contextual understanding and flexibility that humans have, it may make decisions that are technically logical based on its programming but unsuitable or dangerous in real-world contexts.

In healthcare, another area prone to flawed AI decisions, AI models can misinterpret medical data if the training set is incomplete or skewed. For example, if an AI model is trained mostly on data from younger patients, it may struggle to make accurate diagnoses for elderly patients with different symptoms or conditions. This limitation underscores the need to carefully scrutinize AI's recommendations in critical decision-making scenarios where human lives are at stake. Likewise, predictive models used in financial markets may fail during economic crises or unprecedented events because they rely on past data and historical trends, which may not apply to novel situations. In such cases, trusting AI without human judgment can lead to significant financial losses or mismanagement.

Bias in AI models can also lead to flawed outcomes in criminal justice applications, where AI systems are used to predict recidivism rates or determine bail decisions. If these models are trained on biased historical data, such as data reflecting systemic racial disparities in arrests and sentencing, the AI may unfairly disadvantage certain groups, perpetuating unjust outcomes. In such high-stakes situations, where the consequences of AI errors can directly impact human lives and freedom, it's essential to recognize when not to rely solely on AI's judgment.

To mitigate the risks associated with flawed AI decision-making, organizations can take several steps to manage and reduce potential harm:

1. **Ensure Data Diversity and Quality:** The foundation of any AI system is the data it's trained on. To reduce the risk of biased or flawed outputs, it's crucial to use diverse, representative, and high-quality datasets. Data collection should include a broad range of

variables, ensuring that all relevant populations or scenarios are accounted for. In situations where historical data may be biased or incomplete, efforts should be made to clean and correct the data before training AI models. Regular audits of datasets are also necessary to identify potential sources of bias and rectify them before they influence decision-making.

2. **Implement Human Oversight:** AI systems should never be allowed to make critical decisions without human supervision. Human oversight ensures that AI outputs are reviewed and contextualized before any actions are taken. In fields like healthcare, hiring, or criminal justice, human experts must have the final say, validating AI recommendations and making adjustments based on their professional judgment and ethical considerations. By integrating AI as a tool for augmentation rather than as an autonomous decision-maker, organizations can avoid over-reliance on

technology and ensure that AI serves as an aid rather than a replacement for human insight.

3. **Test and Monitor AI Systems Continuously:** AI models are not static—they can drift over time or fail to perform well in changing environments. Continuous testing and monitoring of AI systems are essential to ensure that they are functioning as intended. This includes retraining models regularly to reflect new data, conducting real-world tests to verify their performance, and monitoring their outputs for unexpected behaviors or bias. Performance metrics should be tracked consistently, and any anomalies should be flagged and addressed promptly.

4. **Establish Transparency and Explainability:** One of the main challenges with AI systems is their opacity—often referred to as the "black box" problem. Ensuring that AI systems are transparent and explainable is key to building trust and accountability. Organizations should implement models that

offer clear explanations for their decisions, especially in sensitive areas like finance, healthcare, or law enforcement. Providing transparency around how AI reaches its conclusions allows stakeholders to understand potential weaknesses or biases in the model and empowers them to make better-informed decisions.

5. **Adopt Ethical AI Practices:** Ethical AI development is critical for managing risks and ensuring that AI systems are used responsibly. Organizations should establish ethical guidelines for AI deployment, ensuring that fairness, accountability, and transparency are prioritized throughout the design and implementation process. This includes building systems that are inclusive, reducing bias, and ensuring that the AI is aligned with human values and societal norms. An interdisciplinary approach—bringing in ethicists, social scientists, and legal experts alongside AI developers—can

help organizations anticipate and mitigate unintended consequences.

6. **Utilize Fail-Safes and Escalation Mechanisms:** In scenarios where AI systems make decisions autonomously, it's essential to have fail-safes in place. These could include systems that automatically flag high-risk or unusual decisions for human review or escalation protocols that allow human intervention when AI outputs appear questionable. For instance, if a predictive model in a financial firm suggests an unusual investment strategy, the system could prompt a risk analyst to review the decision before it's implemented. This ensures that AI doesn't operate unchecked and that safeguards are in place to catch errors or misjudgments.

By implementing these risk mitigation strategies, organizations can maximize the benefits of AI while minimizing its potential downsides. While AI has the power to streamline operations, improve decision-making, and drive innovation, its limitations mean that human oversight, ethical considerations, and continuous monitoring remain essential components of any AI-driven process.

Chapter 10: AI Ethics and Policy – Shaping the Future Responsibly

As artificial intelligence continues to permeate nearly every aspect of modern life, the need for ethical AI development and use has become a pressing issue. AI's vast capabilities offer enormous benefits, from improving healthcare outcomes and optimizing business operations to enhancing personalized services and advancing scientific research. However, with this power comes a significant responsibility to ensure that AI is developed and used in ways that are fair, transparent, and aligned with human values. The growing importance of ethics in AI is evident in the increasing focus on addressing bias, ensuring accountability, protecting privacy, and promoting inclusivity in AI systems.

One of the primary ethical concerns in AI is the potential for bias. AI systems, which rely on vast datasets for training, can unintentionally inherit and perpetuate biases present in the data. For example, AI models trained on historical hiring data may reflect the unconscious biases of past decision-makers, leading to discriminatory outcomes in hiring processes. Similarly, in criminal justice, AI systems used to predict recidivism rates have been found to disproportionately target certain racial or socioeconomic groups, resulting in biased sentencing or parole decisions. These examples highlight the ethical dilemma of bias in AI and underscore the need for developers to actively address these issues during the design and training phases of AI systems.

Another critical aspect of ethical AI is accountability. AI systems, especially those used in high-stakes environments like healthcare, finance, or autonomous driving, must be accountable for the decisions they make. However, many AI systems operate as "black boxes," meaning that their internal decision-making processes are opaque and difficult to understand, even for the engineers who created them. This lack of transparency makes it challenging to determine who should be held responsible when AI systems make mistakes or cause harm. For example, if an autonomous vehicle is involved in an accident, determining liability—whether it lies with the car manufacturer, the software developer, or the end user—can be a complex ethical and legal challenge. Ensuring that AI systems are explainable and transparent is crucial to fostering trust and accountability in their use.

Privacy is another key ethical concern in AI development. AI systems, particularly those used in surveillance, advertising, and personalized services, often require access to large amounts of personal data to function effectively. However, the use of this data raises significant privacy concerns, as individuals may not always be aware of how their data is being collected, stored, or used. For instance, AI-driven social media algorithms track user behavior to curate content and target advertisements, often without users fully understanding the extent of the data being collected. The Cambridge Analytica scandal is a stark reminder of how personal data can be exploited by AI systems for unethical purposes. As AI systems become more sophisticated, the need for stringent privacy protections and data governance is critical to prevent the misuse of personal information and to ensure that individuals have control over their data.

Inclusivity in AI is another area that has garnered increasing attention in recent years. AI systems are often designed by teams that may not reflect the diversity of the populations their technologies will affect. This lack of inclusivity can result in AI models that fail to account for the needs and experiences of marginalized or underrepresented groups. For example, facial recognition technology has been shown to perform poorly on people with darker skin tones, largely due to the lack of diversity in the training data. Ensuring that AI development teams are diverse and that the data used to train AI systems is representative of all groups is essential for creating equitable and inclusive AI systems that serve the needs of everyone, not just a select few.

The ethical implications of AI also extend to how the technology is deployed and its impact on society at large. As AI systems become more integrated into the workplace, concerns about job displacement and economic inequality are growing. While AI has the potential to create new opportunities and industries, it is also likely to automate many jobs, disproportionately affecting lower-skilled workers. The ethical challenge here is to ensure that the benefits of AI are distributed fairly across society and that workers who are displaced by automation are provided with opportunities for retraining and upskilling.

Additionally, the ethical use of AI requires careful consideration of its potential to be weaponized or misused. AI has been employed in the development of autonomous weapons and surveillance systems, raising concerns about its potential to violate human rights or be used in harmful ways. For example, AI-powered drones and other autonomous weapons systems can make decisions about targeting without human intervention, raising serious ethical questions about the role of AI in warfare. Similarly, AI-driven surveillance systems, such as China's social credit system, have the potential to infringe on individual freedoms and privacy, leading to concerns about state control and authoritarianism. These examples highlight the need for global ethical standards and regulations to ensure that AI is used in ways that promote peace, human rights, and the public good.

To address these challenges, many organizations and governments are working to develop frameworks and guidelines for the ethical development and use of AI. For instance, the European Union has proposed regulations that focus on creating trustworthy AI systems by ensuring that they are transparent, accountable, and aligned with ethical principles. Similarly, the AI Ethics Guidelines for Trustworthy AI, developed by the European Commission, emphasize the importance of respecting human rights, diversity, and privacy in AI systems. These guidelines call for human oversight, transparency, and fairness in AI, encouraging organizations to build systems that are not only effective but also ethical.

In addition to regulations, fostering a culture of ethical AI development within organizations is essential. Companies that are developing AI technologies should prioritize ethics from the beginning, embedding ethical considerations into the design, training, and deployment phases of AI systems. This might involve establishing internal ethics boards, conducting regular audits of AI systems for bias and fairness, and ensuring that developers are trained in ethical AI practices. By making ethics a core component of AI development, organizations can help ensure that AI technologies are used responsibly and for the benefit of society.

In conclusion, as AI continues to evolve and become more embedded in our daily lives, the importance of ethical AI cannot be overstated. From addressing bias and ensuring accountability to protecting privacy and promoting inclusivity, the ethical challenges posed by AI are numerous and complex. However, by prioritizing ethical considerations in AI development and use, we can harness the power of AI for good, ensuring that it serves as a force for progress, fairness, and human well-being.

As artificial intelligence continues to advance, key ethical concerns around its development and deployment have come to the forefront, including issues related to privacy, bias, and the potential misuse of the technology. These challenges pose significant risks, not just to individuals but also to society as a whole. Understanding and addressing these concerns is essential to ensuring that AI is developed and used responsibly, with a focus on fairness, transparency, and the public good.

One of the most pressing ethical issues in AI is privacy. AI systems often require large amounts of personal data to function effectively, whether they are used in healthcare, marketing, social media, or law enforcement. This raises significant privacy concerns, as individuals may not fully understand how their data is being collected, stored, and used by AI systems. For example, AI-driven algorithms used by social media platforms track user behavior to deliver personalized content and advertisements, often without explicit user consent. Similarly, in healthcare, AI models analyze sensitive patient data to offer diagnostic or treatment recommendations. While these applications can bring tremendous benefits, they also present risks if data is not handled with care. Personal information can be exposed, misused, or exploited by malicious actors, leading to privacy violations and loss of trust in AI systems.

Another major ethical issue is bias in AI. AI models learn from data, and if the data they are trained on reflects existing biases, the models can perpetuate and even amplify these biases. This has been particularly problematic in fields like hiring, criminal justice, and facial recognition. For instance, AI systems used in hiring processes have been shown to favor male candidates over female ones due to biased training data. In the criminal justice system, AI-powered tools designed to predict recidivism rates have been found to disproportionately recommend harsher penalties for individuals from certain racial or ethnic backgrounds. Bias in AI can lead to unfair, discriminatory outcomes, making it crucial to identify and address biases during the development and deployment of AI systems.

The potential misuse of AI technology is another critical ethical concern. AI has the capacity to be weaponized or used for harmful purposes, such as in the development of autonomous weapons, mass surveillance systems, or deepfake technology. Autonomous weapons systems, for example, can make life-or-death decisions without human intervention, raising concerns about accountability and the ethical implications of delegating such decisions to machines. Similarly, AI-driven surveillance tools, while useful for maintaining security, can easily be used to violate individual privacy and freedoms, as seen in cases where governments use AI to monitor and control citizens. Deepfake technology, which uses AI to create convincing but fake audio or video, has also raised concerns about misinformation and its potential to manipulate public opinion or spread false narratives.

Given these ethical challenges, governance and regulation play a vital role in ensuring that AI is developed and used responsibly. Governments and organizations must create frameworks that protect individuals' rights, promote fairness, and mitigate the risks associated with AI technology. In many countries, governments are beginning to recognize the need for comprehensive AI regulations to address the ethical concerns posed by the technology.

One of the most notable efforts in AI governance is the European Union's proposed regulations for trustworthy AI. The EU's approach is focused on establishing clear standards for transparency, accountability, and human oversight in AI systems. These regulations aim to ensure that AI is developed in a way that respects fundamental rights and human dignity. For example, the EU's proposed AI Act includes provisions for high-risk AI systems, such as those used in healthcare, law enforcement, and employment, requiring that they meet strict criteria for fairness, transparency, and reliability. The Act also calls for rigorous testing and monitoring to ensure that AI systems function as intended without causing harm.

The role of organizations in governing AI is equally important. Many companies are now establishing internal frameworks to ensure that AI technologies are developed and deployed ethically. This includes setting up ethics committees, conducting regular audits of AI models for bias, and adopting best practices for data governance and privacy protection. Some organizations have also begun implementing AI "ethics by design," embedding ethical principles into the development process from the outset. This proactive approach ensures that ethical considerations are not an afterthought but are integral to the creation and deployment of AI systems.

International collaboration is also crucial in AI governance. Since AI is a global technology that transcends national borders, its regulation cannot be left to individual countries alone. International organizations such as the United Nations and the Organisation for Economic Co-operation and Development (OECD) are working on creating global frameworks to ensure responsible AI development. These efforts aim to promote cooperation between countries, standardize ethical guidelines, and ensure that AI technologies are used for the benefit of all, rather than exacerbating inequalities or posing new threats.

In addition to formal regulations, fostering a culture of responsible AI use within the tech community is critical. Developers, researchers, and engineers who work on AI technologies must be educated on the ethical implications of their work and be equipped with the tools to create AI systems that prioritize fairness and transparency. This involves not only technical training but also raising awareness about the societal impact of AI and the importance of ethical decision-making throughout the development process.

Moreover, public engagement is essential to building trust in AI. People should be informed about how AI systems affect their lives, particularly when it comes to privacy, fairness, and security. Governments and organizations need to communicate clearly with the public about the benefits and risks of AI, ensuring that individuals have a say in how these technologies are used. This could include public consultations, open debates, and greater transparency about the use of AI in areas like law enforcement, healthcare, and public services.

In conclusion, the growing importance of ethical AI development and governance cannot be overstated. Key ethical concerns such as privacy, bias, and the potential misuse of AI highlight the need for robust regulatory frameworks and a commitment to responsible AI practices. Governments, organizations, and international bodies all play a vital role in ensuring that AI is developed and used in ways that are fair, transparent, and beneficial to society. By addressing these challenges through governance, regulation, and public engagement, we can harness the full potential of AI while safeguarding against its risks, ensuring that AI serves as a tool for positive social and economic impact.

Conclusion

As the world rapidly shifts toward a future dominated by artificial intelligence, the importance of mastering these ten essential AI skills cannot be overstated. AI is no longer a distant concept or a tool reserved for technical experts—it has become an integral part of nearly every industry, driving innovation, optimizing processes, and reshaping the way we live and work. Whether you're looking to stay ahead in your career, grow your business, or simply adapt to the evolving landscape, these AI skills offer the foundation needed to not only keep pace but to lead in this transformative era.

From prompt engineering and AI-powered personal branding to data storytelling and AI strategy execution, each skill plays a crucial role in helping individuals leverage the full potential of AI. The ability to understand and work with AI systems, manage AI projects, and apply AI in creative, strategic, and ethical ways will distinguish the leaders from the followers in the AI-driven economy. By mastering these skills, you position yourself at the forefront of this revolution, ready to seize the opportunities that AI brings.

But this journey does not end with mastering these skills. The AI field is continuously evolving, and staying relevant requires an ongoing commitment to learning, experimentation, and adaptation. AI technologies will keep advancing, and new tools, techniques, and challenges will emerge. Those who succeed in the AI-driven future will be the ones who remain curious, embrace lifelong learning, and are unafraid to explore uncharted territories.

Now is the time to take action. Keep learning, stay curious, and seek out opportunities to apply what you've learned. Engage with AI in your work, test out new tools, and keep expanding your knowledge as AI technologies evolve. Experiment with projects, push the boundaries of your creativity, and remain adaptable in the face of new challenges. The AI revolution is here, and the future belongs to those who are prepared to lead. Embrace these skills, commit to continuous growth, and secure your place as a leader in this rapidly transforming world. The future is full of possibilities, and it's yours to shape.

www.ingramcontent.com/pod-product-compliance
Lightning Source LLC
Chambersburg PA
CBHW050319230526
45471CB00005B/2258